Grammar Girl's™

101 Misused Words You'll Never Confuse Again

Also by Mignon Fogarty

Grammar Girl's™

101 Misused Words You'll Never Confuse Again

MIGNON FOGARTY

ST. MARTIN'S GRIFFIN   NEW YORK

For the confused

GRAMMAR GIRL'S 101 MISUSED WORDS YOU'LL NEVER CONFUSE AGAIN. Copyright © 2011 by Mignon Fogarty, Inc. Grammar Girl is a trademark of Mignon Fogarty, Inc. All rights reserved. Printed in the United States of America. For information, address St. Martin's Press, 175 Fifth Avenue, New York, N.Y. 10010.

www.stmartins.com

Designed by Meryl Sussman Levavi
Illustrations by Arnie Ten

Library of Congress Cataloging-in-Publication Data

Fogarty, Mignon.
    Grammar Girl's 101 misused words you'll never confuse again / Mignon Fogarty.—1st ed.
                p. cm.
    ISBN 978-0-312-57337-9
    1. English language—Usage.   2. English language—Terms and phrases.   3. English language—Errors of usage.   I. Title.   II. Title: 101 misused words you'll never confuse again.
    PE1460.F576 2011
    428.1—dc22

                                        2011011238

First Edition: July 2011

10 9 8 7 6 5 4

Introduction

Ah, English. We have so many words that sound alike but mean different things or take on meanings that don't make sense that it's hard to keep it all straight. Further (or is it farther? you'll find out!), once some people start using a word incorrectly, that use can spread to a point where there's an all-out battle between the people who support what the word is *supposed* to mean and the masses who think it should mean something else.

Sadly, the masses are often unaware that they are even the target of a stickler war. Yet, target they are, and sticklers who will judge you for using the wrong word are lurking everywhere—in your school, your workplace, your family, and your favorite Internet hangout.

A dirty little secret you can invoke to keep you sane is that there are so many confusing words that everyone is part of the "confused masses" for at least a few of them. Many times I've corrected a stickler who actually had something wrong, and

Introduction

I've heard a literate, well-educated person say, "What do you know? I never knew that!" in response to one of my tips. I've also made mistakes myself—for example, I grew up saying *snuck* instead of *sneaked* and didn't know it was controversial until someone corrected me and I looked it up myself. So don't be ashamed if you get confused. The only reason to be ashamed is if you are too lazy to find out what is right once you suspect you might be wrong.

In this book, I've highlighted 101 troublesome words that people often confuse, and I've tried to give you fun and easy ways to remember what they mean. Since they're usually problematic word pairs, you're actually getting tips for almost 200 words. Quite a bonus for a book titled *101 Words* . . . , eh?

A Versus An

Sadly, a lot of people were taught the wrong rule for using the articles **a** and **an**. It's the sound of the next word that determines the word choice, not the first letter.

If the next word starts with a vowel *sound*, use *an*. If the next word starts with a consonant *sound*, use *a*. That means a word starting with *u* or *o*, for example, can require *a* or *an* depending on the pronunciation: a unicorn, an uncle, a onetime deal, an owner.

QUICK AND DIRTY TIP

To remember that words starting with certain letters can go either way, set the image in your mind of a man playing a ukulele under an umbrella—an image that uses two *u*-words that require different articles.

Adieu Versus Ado

Every time I use the word **ado** in a Scrabble game with my husband, he insists it's not a word. He is wrong, but he's not alone. People often incorrectly write *without further adieu* instead of the proper phrase *without further ado*.

Adieu is a French word meaning *farewell*. It's just another way to say good-bye—like *adios* or *ciao*. To mean *good-bye* is how Julie Andrews used *adieu* in the song "So Long, Farewell" in *The Sound of Music*.

An ado, on the other hand, is a hubbub, bustle, flurry, or fuss. You may remember the word *ado* from the title of Shakespeare's comedy *Much Ado About Nothing,* in which a big fuss (an ado) is made about an affair that didn't happen.

In some instances, it is understandable that people could mistakenly believe the meaning of *adieu* makes sense in *without further adieu*. For example, if dinner guests want to leave without further excessive farewells, it may seem logical to say something such as "Without further adieu, we're off to the movies." Logical, but incorrect. If that is your sentiment, you need to use the plural: *adieus*.

Advice Versus Advise

The main difference between **advice** and **advise** is that *advice* is a noun and *advise* is a verb—the act of giving advice.

> **You once told me, don't get emotional about stock. Don't! The bid is 16 ½ and going down. As your broker, I** advise **you to take it.**
>
> Charlie Sheen playing Bud Fox
in the movie Wall Street

Advice, meaning an opinion about what should be done, is an abstract noun. It isn't something solid you can see, but it's a noun nonetheless. Other abstract nouns include *courage* and *loyalty.*

> **Let me give you a nickel's worth of free** advice **young man. This so-called Dr. Brown is dangerous; he's a real nutcase. You hang around with him, you're gonna end up in big trouble.**
>
> —James Tolkan playing Mr. Strickland
in the movie Back to the Future

QUICK AND DIRTY TIP

Advice ends in *ice,* and it's easy to remember that a block of ice is a noun. (Even though the *ice* in *advice* has nothing to do with frozen water, thinking of it that way can help you remember which word to use.)

Aesthetics
Versus Ascetics

Ascetics are people who live an extremely simple life, usually characterized by the rejection of material possessions and worldly pleasures. *Ascetic* is related to the Greek name for a monk or a hermit (*askētēs*) and the Greek word meaning "to exercise or train" (*askein*).

> **Throughout history power has been the vice of the** ascetic.
>
> —Bertrand Russell, a British philosopher

The concept of **aesthetics** is a bit more difficult to define but generally relates to beauty or how something affects the senses. For example, a room can have good *aesthetics* or bad *aesthetics*. *Aesthetics* is also a branch of philosophy that considers such things.

Most people probably wouldn't be pleased with the *aesthetics* of an *ascetic*'s home. You may sometimes see the word spelled *esthetics*. That spelling is considered an acceptable variant in American English, but *aesthetics* is still the standard spelling in Britain and the preferred spelling in America.

> **Don't talk to me about** aesthetics **or tradition. Talk to me about what sells and what's good right now.**
>
> —George Steinbrenner, former owner of the New York Yankees

Affect Versus Effect

Most of the time, **affect** is a verb and **effect** is a noun.

Affect most commonly means something like "to influence" or "to change." *Affect* can also mean, roughly, "to act in a way you don't feel," as in *He affected an air of superiority.*

> **I'd like to see some sign that it** affects **you or that you recognize that it** affects **other people.**
>
> —Omar Epps playing Dr. Eric Foreman
> in the TV show *House*

Effect has a lot of subtle meanings as a noun, but to me the meaning "a result" seems to be at the core of all the definitions.

> **When I see** effects **and I'm unable to discern the cause, my faith in reason and consequence is shaken.**
>
> —Emily Deschanel playing Dr. Temperance Brennan
> in the TV show *Bones*

Affect Versus Effect

In rare instances, the roles are switched. For example, you can *effect* change (a verb) and display a happy *affect* (a noun). (In the latter case, *affect* means "an emotion or disposition"—shown either on your face or in your body language.

QUICK AND DIRTY TIP

Affect is usually an action (both start with *a*). Like most nouns, you can usually put an article (*the* or *an*) in front of *effect* without ruining the meaning of the sentence.

Affective
Versus Effective

Even when people understand the difference between affect and effect, they often still get confused about **affective** and **effective**.

If you're trying to decide between the two, *effective* is almost always the right choice. Its synonyms include *forceful*, *powerful*, *useful*, *capable,* and *taking effect.*

> **Based on your cost in materials and your wholesale selling price, you'll** effectively **be paying yourself five dollars and nineteen cents a day.**
>
> —Jim Parsons playing Sheldon Cooper
> in the TV show *The Big Bang Theory*

> Effective **immediately, I am shutting down the weapons manufacturing division of Stark Industries.**
>
> —Robert Downey Jr. playing Tony Stark
> in the movie *Iron Man*

Affective relates to emotions; you're most likely to hear it as the name of a psychological condition such as seasonal *affective* disorder (in which a type of depression is triggered by the decrease in sunlight in the winter).

Allude Versus Elude

Allude and **elude** sound similar and share the same Latin root word, but they don't mean the same thing.

Allude means "to refer to indirectly."

> **No jokes. No innuendos, no quips. Don't even think of** alluding **to having seen me naked or having touched any part of my body that does not have fingers.**
>
> —Kristen Bell playing Veronica Mars in the TV show *Veronica Mars*

Elude means "to avoid, evade, or escape."

> **The Neutrinos have** eluded **us.**
>
> —A rock soldier in the TV show *Teenage Mutant Ninja Turtles*

QUICK AND DIRTY TIP

Remember that *elude*, *escape*, and *evade* all start with the letter *e*.

Altar Versus Alter

An **altar** is a place, often an elevated place such as a table, used for religious rites or spiritual offerings. The word arose in English around the year A.D. 1000, which is surprisingly recent given its tie to religion.

> **In this bar I will always be known as the guy who was left at the** altar**. It sucks.**
>
> —Josh Radnor playing Ted Mosby
> in the TV show *How I Met Your Mother*

Alter is a more recent word, dating from the fourteenth century and coming from the Latin word for "other." It means to change or modify.

> **If you ever travel back in time, don't step on anything. Because even the slightest change can** alter **the future in ways you can't imagine.**
>
> —Dan Castellaneta voicing Grandpa Simpson
> in the TV show *The Simpsons*

QUICK AND DIRTY TIP

Religious people often talk about putting God first in their lives, and *a* is the first letter of the alphabet. That can help you remember that the object used for religious rites is spelled *altar*.

Anniversary

Anniversary should be reserved for something that happens once a year, but people often use it incorrectly to refer to something that happens weekly or monthly. New lovers are annoying enough without also butchering the language to talk about their three-week *anniversary*.

Anniversary comes from two Latin words: *annus,* which means "year," and *vertere,* which means "to turn." So an *anniversary* is literally the turning of a year—not something that should be attached to weeks or months.

> **This is the seventy-fifth** anniversary
> **issue. There is only going to be one**
> **seventy-fifth** anniversary **issue ever, and it's**
> **on our watch. We screw this up and we**
> **basically mooned a piece of history.**
>
> —Liza Weil playing Paris Geller
> in the TV show *Gilmore Girls*

Filipino English speakers seem to have a better grasp of the limitations of the word *anniversary* than Americans; I'm told *monthsary* is a common term in the Philippines for describing monthly landmarks.

QUICK AND DIRTY TIP

Remember that *anniversary* is related to the the word *annual*.

Anxious Versus Eager

Anxious comes from a Latin word that means "worried, uneasy, or distressed"; and **eager** comes from a Latin word that means "sharp or keen."

To some, *anxious* has more of a negative connotation than *eager*. You're *eager* for your long-distance boyfriend's plane to arrive—unless you're going to break up with him; then you're more likely to be *anxious* for his plane to arrive so you can get it over with. *Anxious* is evolving, though: the distinction between the two terms was much stronger in the seventeenth century. Today, many people use the words interchangeably.

> **I think everything must go back to the fact that I had a very** anxious **childhood. My mother never had time for me. You know, when you're . . . the middle child in a family of five million, you don't get any attention.**
>
> —Woody Allen as Z in the movie *Antz*

> **Well, I don't wanna seem too** eager. **One Mississippi, two Mississippi, that seems good.**
>
> —Matt LeBlanc as Joey Tribbiani
> in the TV show *Friends*

QUICK AND DIRTY TIP

If you wish to make a distinction between *anxious* and *eager*, think of Xanax, the anti-*anxiety* drug with all those *x*'s, as a way to remember that *anxious* conveys a sense of being distraught.

Assume Versus Presume

If you **assume** something about someone, you're basing your information on nothing—no facts or proof, just your belief gathered from thin air.

> **Before a man speaks, it is always safe to** assume **that he is a fool. After he speaks, it is seldom necessary to** assume **it.**
>
> —H. L. Mencken, author of
> *The American Language*

If you **presume** to know something about someone, that presumption is based on evidence or facts.

> **We falsely attribute to men a determined character; putting together all their yesterdays, and averaging them, we** presume **we know them.**
>
> —Henry David Thoreau, author of *Walden*

QUICK AND DIRTY TIP

You have likely heard the famous quotation "Dr. Livingstone, I *presume*." This line was spoken by Sir Henry Morton, who was a reporter in 1871 when he went to Africa in search of the aforementioned missionary and explorer, Dr. David Livingstone. He used *presume* because he *expected* the person he encountered to be Dr. Livingstone.

Astrologer
Versus Astronomer

What's the quickest way to insult **astronomers**? Call them **astrologers**.

Astronomers are scientists who study space and things in space such as planets, moons, stars, suns, and asteroids. An *astronomer* might say, "An increase in solar flare activity will increase the intensity and duration of the Northern Lights this weekend."

Astrologers make predictions about human activities and proclivities based on the positions and movements of celestial bodies. An *astrologer* might say, "You're an Aries and she's a Leo; you belong together!"

> **I'm a Gemini, and Geminis don't believe in astrology.**
>
> —Clive Owen, playing Jack in the movie *Croupier*

QUICK AND DIRTY TIP

Astronomers are scientists who discover new planets. Therefore, *astronomers* must name new planets. *Astronomer* ends with *nomer,* which sounds a lot like *namer.* Astro<u>nomer</u>s are the <u>namer</u>s of new planets. On the other hand, *astrologers* observe and work with only the current known heavenly bodies—no naming involved. (This memory trick is not based on the true origins of the words, but it helps me remember the difference between *astrologers* and *astronomers*.)

Bad Versus Badly

Bad is an adjective and **badly** is an adverb, so usually you use *badly* to modify a verb because most verbs are action verbs:

> **No, I don't think I will kiss you, although you need kissing,** badly.
>
> —Clark Gable playing Rhett Butler in the movie *Gone with the Wind*

There's an exception, though—you use *bad* to modify linking verbs such as *be, is,* and *was:*

> **What Saleem did was** bad **enough. Becoming like him would be worse.**
>
> —Cote de Pablo playing Ziva David in the TV show *NCIS: Naval Criminal Investigative Service*

When you're talking about your emotions, the right thing to say is that you feel *bad,* not that you feel *badly,* because *feel* is a linking verb when it refers to your emotions rather than your sense of touch.

QUICK AND DIRTY TIP

If you can replace a verb with a form of *to be* (such as *is* or *was*) without dramatically changing the meaning of the sentence, it is a linking verb.

Baited Versus Bated

Bated is one of the many words Shakespeare invented (or at least he was the first person to put the word on a piece of paper that survived to this day so that dictionary makers could find it). **Baited** is the past tense of the word *bait*, meaning "to lure an animal or person." The reason these two words confuse people is because of the phrase *with bated breath*.

Bated is a form of *abate*, which means "to diminish, beat down, or reduce." So when you're waiting with *bated* (read: abated) breath, you're so eager, anxious, excited, or frightened that you're almost holding your breath.

Shakespeare used the phrase *with bated breath* in *The Merchant of Venice* in a scene where Shylock (the moneylender) points out the irony of Antonio (the merchant) coming to him for a loan after Antonio treated him so poorly in the past:

> **Shall I bend low and in a bondman's key,**
> **With bated breath and whispering**
> **   humbleness, Say this;**
> **"Fair sir, you spit on me on Wednesday last;**
> **You spurn'd me such a day; another time**
> **You call'd me dog; and for these courtesies**
> **I'll lend you thus much moneys"?**

Since *bated* is a word many modern people don't know, it's common to see *with bated breath* incorrectly written as *with baited breath*.

There's an odd logic to the *baited* misunderstanding—you *bait* a hook to catch a fish, and people eagerly waiting for something could be tempted to put out metaphorical *bait,* but why would it be their breath? It wouldn't. Nobody would rush toward fishy breath.

Simply remember the moneylender Shylock and his abated breath.

Because Of
Versus Due To

When you're choosing between **because of** and **due to**, *because of* is almost always the better choice. For example, it's best to say, "I don't have any homework *because of* [not *due to*] the holiday," and "*Because of* [not *due to*] the holiday, I don't have any homework."

> **I personally think we developed language** because of **our deep need to complain.**
>
> —Lily Tomlin, American comedian

It's best to reserve *due to* for times when you mean "owed" or "expected." For example, "He sent the money that was *due to* her," or "She was *due to* arrive at noon."

> **Have you not met Will Turner? He's noble, heroic—terrific soprano. Worth at least four . . . maybe three and a half. And did I happen to mention . . . he's in love? With a girl.** Due to **be married. Betrothed. Dividing him from her and her from him would only be half as cruel as actually allowing them to be joined in holy matrimony, eh?**
>
> —Johnny Depp playing Jack Sparrow in the movie *Pirates of the Caribbean: Dead Man's Chest*

Beck and Call Versus Beckon Call

The correct phrase is **beck and call**, not **beckon call**. If you are at people's *beck and call*, you respond immediately whether they beckon or call; it implies complete subservience.

Beck and call goes back to the late 1800s—a time when *beck* meant *beckon*. Archaic words or word forms can continue to be used in set phrases, as we saw with *bated breath* [p. 18], long after they've fallen out of favor in everyday language.

> **EDWARD: I will pay you to be at my beck and call.**
>
> **VIVIAN: Look, I'd love to be your beck-and-call girl, but . . .**
>
> —Richard Gere and Julia Roberts
> in the movie *Pretty Woman*

QUICK AND DIRTY TIP

Remember that it's three words and not two by thinking that if you're at someone's *beck and call*, he or she will always want you to do more (and three words is more than two).

Born Versus Borne

Born and **borne** are both past tense forms (past participles) of the verb *to bear*.

Use *born* to write about someone or something entering the world, or when you're using the word as an adjective, as in Nevada's nickname: the Battle Born State.

> **Be not afraid of greatness: some men are** born **great, some achieve greatness, and some have greatness thrust upon 'em.**
>
> —Malvalio in William Shakespeare's play
> *Twelfth Night*

Use *borne* in almost every other instance—for example, to write about carrying something or enduring something.

> **Alas, poor Yorick! I knew him, Horatio: a fellow of infinite jest, of most excellent fancy. He hath** borne **me on his back a thousand times.**
>
> —Hamlet in William Shakespeare's play *Hamlet*

QUICK AND DIRTY TIP

When a baby or an idea enters the world, it is small, just as *born* is the smaller of the two words.

Breath _Versus_ Breathe

The word **breath**, which originally meant any vapor or smell that was released or exhaled from something hot (such as steam from a cooking pot), came first; it was followed by **breathe** a few centuries later. Today, _breath_ means the air inhaled or exhaled when you _breathe,_ which means inhaling or exhaling air. Most people use these words correctly when they speak; it's when they write them that they get it wrong.

> **While I appreciate the "Oh, snap!" I don't like your moist** breath **on my ear.**
>
> —Jim Parsons playing Sheldon Cooper on the TV show _The Big Bang Theory_

> **No, we have to take in nourishment, expel waste, and** breathe **in enough oxygen to keep our cells from dying. Everything else is purely optional.**
>
> —Jim Parsons playing Sheldon Cooper on the TV show _The Big Bang Theory_

QUICK AND DIRTY TIP

The word with the strong hard _e_ sound is the one with the _e_ on the end: _breathe._

Cache Versus Cachet

Cache is pronounced like *cash* and is the name for a place to store or hide things. It's also a type of computer memory where things are stored for fast retrieval.

> **There were so many missing pieces. I was starting to find some of them, working my way upriver, collecting a secret** cache **of broken memories in a shoebox.**

> —*White Oleander* by Janet Fitch

Cachet is a type of importance, prestige, or status. For example, you can say a restaurant has a certain *cachet* to explain that it is fancy and special. It's also an official seal on a document (and note how having an official seal makes a document important or prestigious).

"As Patron-Sponsor, I am charged with . . ."—he paused and consulted the notes—"adding a sense of royal cachet **to proceedings today." He waited while a ripple of conversation ran around the room. Nobody was quite sure what adding a sense of royal** cachet **really meant. But everyone agreed that it sounded impressive indeed.**

Erak's Ransom by John Flanagan

Cache and *cachet* both come from a French word that means "to hide or conceal." *Cachet* was used in English much earlier, and *cache* may have evolved later from the slang French Canadian trappers used to describe the places they kept their stores.

QUICK AND DIRTY TIP

You can remember that *cachet* means important and prestigious by thinking the *t* represents the cross the pope wears around his neck.

Capital Versus Capitol

When the noun ends with an *ol,* it's referring to buildings—state **capitol** buildings or the *Capitol* building in Washington, D.C. You can remember that the rotunda of the D.C. *Capitol* building is round like the letter *o.*

> **Oh my God, it's** Capitol **Barbie.**
>
> —J. Barton playing Timothy McGinn
> in the movie *Legally Blonde 2:*
> *Red White & Blonde*

Capital refers to (among other things) uppercase letters, wealth, lethal punishment, or a city that is the seat of government for its region or is important in some way.

> **Nobody tries to plead guilty in a** capital
> **case.**
>
> —Byrne Piven playing Benny Conway in the movie
> *The A-Team* (a *capital* case is one that involves
> the death penalty)

QUICK AND DIRTY TIP

Don't get confused by the fact that *capital* with an *al* is used for a *capital* city and *capitol* with an *ol* is used for a *capitol* building. Just remember the *o* is round like a building's rotunda.

Carat, Caret, Carrot, and Karat

Carrot, likely derived from the Greek word for "head," is an orange root plant. *Carrots* and *Carrot Top* are also nicknames for people with red hair.

Gems such as diamonds are weighed in a unit called a **carat**, which equals 200 milligrams. The largest cut diamond in the world is the Golden Jubilee Diamond, which was found in South Africa and weighs nearly 550 *carats*.

> **I never worry about diets. The only carrots that interest me are the number of** carats **in a diamond.**
>
> —Mae West

The purity of gold in an alloy is measured in a proportional unit called a **karat**. Pure gold is 24 *karats*.

A **caret** is an insertion mark: ^

Chute Versus Shoot

Chute comes from an Old French word that meant "to fall." It sounds French if you think about it. It reminds me of *chignon, chantilly,* and *champagne.* A *chute* is something such as a slide or shaft that helps people or things make a safe, controlled descent.

> **Someone has to save our skins. Into the garbage** chute, **fly boy.**
>
> —Princess Leia to Han Solo in *Star Wars: Episode IV—A New Hope*

Shoot is a very old word that goes at least as far back as Old English and has more than fifty different definitions—"to go quickly," "to sprout (plants)," "to send a bullet through the air," and so on.

> **You'll** shoot **your eye out.**
>
> —Multiple adults to Ralphie in *The Christmas Story* explaining why he can't have a Red Ryder BB gun

QUICK AND DIRTY TIP

Most people would recognize that parachute is spelled *parachute*, not *parashoot*. Think of a parachute as something that helps people fall safely from the sky, and think of *chute* as a shortened version of *parachute*.

Cite Versus
Sight Versus Site

Cite is an important word to know for writing papers. When you quote people, always *cite* them—attribute the quotation to them. *Cite* comes from an Old French word that meant "to summon."

A **site** is a location or place such as a work *site* or a Web *site*. The word can also be a verb that means to put something in position. It comes from the Latin word meaning "place "or "position."

Sight refers to the ability to see. It's a long-established English word, coming to us from an Old English word that also meant "sight."

QUICK AND DIRTY TIP

People are less likely to misspell *citation*, so remember that the verb *cite* is related to the noun *citation*.

Complement
Versus Compliment

A **compliment** (with an *i*) is a kind or flattering remark.

> **Come on,** compliment **me. Tell me my hair looks beautiful!**
>
> —Blake Lively playing Serena van der Woodsen in the TV show *Gossip Girl*

A **complement** (with an *e*) is a full crew or set, and when something *complements* something else, it means they go well together.

> **I have [picture frames] custom-made to** complement **each particular piece.**
>
> —Edward Mulhare playing Amory Gilliam in the TV show *The Streets of San Francisco*

> **That's our ship. That's Voyager: Intrepid class, sustainable cruise velocity of warp factor 9.975; fifteen decks; crew** complement **of 141; bio-neural circuitry.**
>
> —Alicia Coppola playing Lieutenant Stadi in the TV show *Star Trek: Voyager*

QUICK AND DIRTY TIP

Be a nice person and tell yourself "I like to give *compliments.*" The *I* in that sentence can remind you that *compliment* is spelled with an *i*.

Compose
Versus Comprise

Collections either **comprise** a list of their parts or are **composed** of their parts.

Compose comes from the Old French words *composer*, which meant "to arrange or put together." It means to make up the parts of something. Think of a musical composer bringing together the parts for all the different instruments to *compose* a symphony.

A full deck is usually composed **of 52 cards.**

Comprise comes from a French word that means "include." In English, it can mean "to include, contain, consist of, and constitute."

52 cards usually comprise **a full deck.**

QUICK AND DIRTY TIP

Compose is almost always the word you want, but when in doubt, remember that the word *of* only comes after *composed*, never after *comprised*. Think that the two o's in c*o*mp*o*sed mean it's the word that goes with *of*.

Conscience
Versus Conscious

You have something on your **conscience** when you feel guilty. Your *conscience* tells you the difference between right and wrong.

> **A lot of people mistake a short memory for a clear** conscience.
>
> —Syndicated newspaper columnist Doug Larson

You are **conscious** when you are awake and *conscious* of something when you are aware of it.

> **Happiness is not achieved by the** conscious **pursuit of happiness; it is generally the by-product of other activities.**
>
> —Novelist Aldous Huxley in an article for *Vedanta and the West,* a journal related to Hindu philosophy and consciousness

---

QUICK AND DIRTY TIP

To remember the spelling of the word that has to do with right and wrong, picture Albert Einstein—a physicist concerned with both science and philosophy—nagging you to do the right thing. The man of <u>science</u> appeals to your con<u>science</u>.

Counsel Versus Council

Counsel is a verb that means "to give advice" (and a noun describing the advice received as a result of counseling).

> **ROBERT LANGDON: You will** counsel **him wisely.**
>
> **CARDINAL STRAUSS: I am an old man. I will** counsel **him briefly.**
>
> —Tom Hanks playing Robert Langdon and Armin Mueller-Stahl playing Cardinal Strauss in the movie *Angels & Demons*

Council is a noun that describes a group of decision makers.

> **You just took a** council **ax from a** council **van, and now you're tearing up a** council **road! I'm reporting you to the** council**!**
>
> —Abdul Salis playing Kel in the TV show *Doctor Who*

QUICK AND DIRTY TIP

Think of the *sel* on the end of *counsel* as similar to *sell*—another verb, an action. Salespeople may try to *counsel* you so they can <u>sell</u> a certain product.

Currant Versus Current

A **currant** is a fruit similar to a raisin. *Currant* comes from the name of the town from which these "raisins of Corauntz" were commonly exported in the fourteenth century.

> **Certain it is that scandal is good brisk talk, whereas praise of one's neighbour is by no means lively hearing. An acquaintance grilled, scored, devilled, and served with mustard and cayenne pepper excites the appetite; whereas a slice of cold friend with** currant **jelly is but a sickly, unrelishing meat.**
>
> —William Makepeace Thackeray, Victorian English writer, in his essay "On a Hundred Years Hence"

Current has many meanings. As an adjective it has to do with the prevailing time or prevalence. As a noun, it is something that flows, such as water in a river or electricity along a wire.

> **On matters of style, swim with the** current, **on matters of principle, stand like a rock.**
>
> —Thomas Jefferson, American president

QUICK AND DIRTY TIP

Curr<u>ant</u>, the food, ends with <u>ant</u>, and ants eat food.

Deep-Seated

Versus Deep-Seeded

Is your belief that zombies will be part of Armageddon a **deep-seated belief** or a **deep-seeded belief**?

The correct phrase is *deep-seated,* even if those zombie beliefs are a bit questionable.

Seat can mean a location, as in "the county seat," or a body part that is the center of some emotion or function. Dictionary.com and the *American Heritage Dictionary* both use the example sentence "The heart is the seat of passion" and the *Oxford English Dictionary* includes an 1850 quotation from *The Method of Divine Government* by James McCosh: "We regard the will as the seat of all virtue and vice."

We don't often use *seat* that way anymore, so it's easy to see why people get confused about *deep-seated.* When you're thinking of something deeply felt or buried, it's not far-fetched to think of a seed buried in the dirt. Nevertheless, *deep-seated* is the right choice. *Deep-seeded* is a mistake.

Defuse Versus Diffuse

Bombs are **defused**—deactivated.

It's easy to see that *de-fuse* literally means to remove the fuse from a bomb.

> **You're the one man that might be able to defuse that bomb.**
>
> —Lee Majors playing Steve Austin in the
> TV show *The Six Million Dollar Man*

Diffuse comes from a Latin word that means "to spread around or pour out." Things that are *diffused* are spread out. For example, odors are *diffused* through a room and light can be *diffused* by a filter or a screen.

> **Wit is as sharp as a stroke of lightning, whereas humor is diffuse like sunlight.**
>
> —Charles S. Brooks, American essayist

These words often get misused when talking about a brouhaha. Do you *defuse* an explosive situation or *diffuse* an explosive situation? Typically, one would speak of *defusing* anger as though it were a bomb, so you would *defuse* an angry mob by giving them pizza—not *diffuse* them with pizza.

Desert Versus Dessert

A **dessert** is something you eat—usually sweet and usually at the end of a meal. It comes from a French word that means "to clear the table."

> **Meat on a dessert? That is not possible.**
>
> —David Schwimmer playing Ross
> on the TV show *Friends*

A **desert** is a dry region with few plants. In the movies, people often cross the *desert* on camels and are rescued just before they die of dehydration. *Desert* comes from a Latin word that means "abandon."

> **God is teasing me. Just like he teased Moses in the** desert.
>
> —Dan Castellaneta voicing Homer Simpson
> in the TV show *The Simpsons*

As a verb, *desert* means to abandon or leave without intending to return.

Desert Versus Dessert

Wondering about the phrase *get your just deserts*? The *desert* in this phrase has a different origin—a French word that means "deserve," and so the phrase means getting what you deserve even though the word is pronounced like *dessert*.

QUICK AND DIRTY TIP

Since food is sparse in a *desert* and you have *dessert* when you're eating a big meal, think of the extra *s* in *dessert* as representing the plentiful bounty of food during a meal with *dessert*.

Disinterested Versus Uninterested

An **uninterested** person is bored, unconcerned, or indifferent.

> **I just don't get it. She seems totally**
> uninterested **in me, despite my smothering**
> **obsessiveness.**
>> —Chris Elliott playing Nathaniel Mayweather
>> in the movie *Cabin Boy*

A **disinterested** person is impartial, unbiased, or has no stake in the outcome.

> **Law is not as** disinterested **as our concepts**
> **of law pretend; law serves power.**
>> —William Sloane Coffin, American clergyman

If you're on trial, you want a *disinterested* judge. Unless you're a laywer, the word you're usually looking for is *uninterested*.

e.g. Versus i.e.

I.e and e.g. are both abbreviations for Latin terms. People often use them interchangeably, but they mean different things.

E.g. stands for *exempli gratia*, which means "for example," so you use it to introduce an example:

> **There are so many different well-formed ways to say the same basic thing, from** e.g. **"I was attacked by a bear!" to "Goddamn bear tried to kill me!" to "That ursine juggernaut did essay to sup upon my person!" and so on.**
>
> —David Foster Wallace, American writer

I.e. stands for *id est* and means roughly "that is" or "in other words," so you use it to introduce a further clarification:

> **The number of guests at dinner should not be less than the number of Graces nor exceed that of the Muses,** i.e., **it should begin with three and stop at nine.**
>
> —Marcus Terentius Varro, Roman writer

QUICK AND DIRTY TIP

Think of *e.g.* being pronounced as *egg* and being the first syllable in *example* (egg-sample). Think of the *i* in *i.e.* as the first letter of *in other words*.

Especially Versus Specially

This was an **especially** fun tip to write; it was **specially** designed for your enjoyment. Does that help you see the difference between *especially* and *specially*?

Especially usually means "particularly."

> **Samantha didn't believe in monogamy,** especially **when it came to real estate agents.**
>
> —Sarah Jessica Parker playing Carrie Bradshaw in
> the TV show *Sex and the City*

Specially usually means "in a special or careful manner" or "specifically."

> **PETER GRIFFIN: Uh, excuse me, I'm Mel Gibson, here for the key to my** specially **reserved room.**
>
> **GUY: You're Mel Gibson?**
>
> **PETER GRIFFIN: Yes, I've put on a few pounds for my next role. I play Peter Griffin, a heroic warrior who defied the English to free England from the English.**
>
> **GUY: Holy mackerel! Let me show you to your room, Mr. Gibson!**
>
> —Seth McFarlane voicing Peter Griffin
> in the TV show *Family Guy*

Explicit Versus Implicit

Something said explicitly is said outright. Think of **explicit** language (words that graphically describe sex or violence), or the "*explicit*" tag on podcasts—not much is left to the imagination.

> **Marty, I gave you** explicit **instructions not to come here but to go directly back to 1985.**
>
> —Christopher Lloyd playing Doc in the movie *Back to the Future Part III*

Something that is **implicit**, or implied, on the other hand, isn't said directly but is known through other actions.

> **Once the** implicit **aim of biography was to uplift, now it is to unveil.**
>
> —Mark Feeney, Pulitzer Prize–winning *Boston Globe* arts critic

The Latin words from which we get *explicit* and *implicit*—*expliticus* and *impliticus*—have the same root. The prefix *ex-* means "out" or "away from," and the prefix *im-* means "not," so *explicit* words are spoken or written out and *implicit* words are not spoken or written.

Implicit can also mean "unquestioningly or without doubt," as in "I trust him implicitly."

Farther Versus Further

Farther refers to physical distance and **further** refers to metaphorical, or figurative, distance.

> **Prof. Robert Crawford: Perhaps your skills do reach** farther **than basketball.**
>
> **Jamal:** "Further."
>
> **Prof. Robert Crawford: What?**
>
> **Jamal: You said that my skills reached** "farther" **than basketball.** "Farther" **relates to distance,** "further" **is a definition of degree. You should have said** "further."
>
> **Prof. Robert Crawford: Are you challenging me, Mr. Wallace?**
>
> —Rob Brown (Jamal) and F. Murray Abraham (Professor Crawford) in the movie *Finding Forrester*

Sometimes it's not so straightforward. If I've read more of a book than you have, I could be *farther* along (in pages) or *further* along (in the story). When it's ambiguous like that, you can use either word.

QUICK AND DIRTY TIP

Remember that *farther* has the word *far* in it, and something that is far is usually some physical distance away.

Faze Versus Phase

Faze is an Americanism just like *OK* (which comes from a jocular misspelling: *oll korrekt*) and *ornery* (which comes from *ordinary*). *Faze* emerged in the 1920s as a variation of the word *feeze* (sometimes spelled *feaze* or *pheese*), which I bet you've never heard before. *Feeze* is an extremely old English word that meant "to beat away, frighten, or drive off"; similarly, *faze* means "to disturb, daunt, or worry":

> **The Hawaiian football team pretended to be** unfazed **when the Minnesota players warmed up shirtless in the snowstorm.**

A **phase**, on the other hand, is most commonly a period or stage such as the *phase* of the moon, the latest leg-warmer fashion *phase*, or the first *phase* of a villain's evil plan. *Phase* comes from the Latin word *phasis,* which means "to bring light or to show" (as in the way the moon or a star shows up in the sky or brings light).

> **Honey, this is just a** phase. **Every teenager goes through it. I did, your father did; Francis cried in the shower every day for six months. Reese wouldn't get out of the dryer. It's awkward, and it's painful, you think it's never going to end. Now get out of bed. We're going to the zoo.**
>
> —Jane Kaczmarek playing Lois
> in the TV show *Malcolm in the Middle*

Fewer Versus Less

Fewer is for things you can count, such as french fries, finches, fireflies, and fritters—one french fry, two finches, three fireflies, four fritters.

> **NILES: Have you noticed there are** fewer **hazlenuts in these biscotti? And yet they've gone up twenty-five cents.**
>
> **FRASIER: Oh,** fewer **nuts, more money— something I've been aspiring to for my entire professional life!**
>
> —David Hyde Pierce playing Niles and Kelsey Grammer playing Frasier in the TV show *Frasier*

Less is for things you can't count, such as love, laughter, loneliness, and laundry.

> **There's not a lot of money in free music. Even** less **when you're being sued by everyone who's ever been invited to the Grammys.**
>
> —Justin Timberlake playing Sean Parker in the movie *The Social Network*

45

Fictional Versus Fictitious

Fictional and **fictitious** are both adjectives that mean roughly "made up" or "invented." The difference between the two is how they are typically used rather than what they mean.

Fictional is usually used to describe something in literature such as a fictional character or a fictional story.

> **If you will practice being** fictional **for a while, you will understand that fictional characters are sometimes more real than people with bodies and heartbeats.**
>
> —Richard Bach, American author of
> *Jonathan Livingston Seagull*

Fictitious is usually used to describe a lie or an invention that happens in real life.

> **Sane and intelligent human beings . . . carefully and cautiously and diligently conceal their private real opinions from the world and give out** fictitious **ones in their stead for general consumption.**
>
> —*Mark Twain in Eruption: Hitherto Unpublished Pages About Men and Events* by Mark Twain

Flack Versus Flak

Flak comes from a German acronym for a type of cannon that shot down airplanes during World War II, so when someone gives you flak, you're metaphorically taking fire.

> **I want you to clean your room, and don't give me any** flak.

Flack arose around the same time as *flak* but is an informal name for a publicity agent or press agent. Some sources say it started as a reference to a successful movie publicity agent named Gene Flack. Today, it's often used in an insulting manner.

> **Did that** flack **send another e-mail about his client's new dog-costume book?**

Flair Versus Flare

Flare comes from an Old English word meaning "to spread or burst out." You light *flares* to attract attention in an emergency, solar *flares* cause electrical problems, and your nostrils may *flare* when you're upset.

> **Don't pander to me, kid. One tiny crack in the hull and our blood boils in thirteen seconds. Solar** flare **might crop up, cook us in our seats.**
>
> —Karl Urban playing Bones
> in the 2009 movie *Star Trek*

Flair comes from an Old French word for "scent." It has a couple of meanings. It can describe a unique or smart style. A chic dresser has *flair*. *Flair* also means natural talent. If you have a *flair* for languages you have a knack for languages.

> **For people without emotion, you sure have a** flair **for the dramatic.**
>
> —Connor Trinneer playing Commander Tucker
> in the TV show *Star Trek: Enterprise*,
> addressing a Vulcan

Flesh Out
Versus Flush Out

Flesh out and **flush out** are both English expressions, but they mean different things. How confusing!

When you develop a project—putting more meat on its bones, so to speak—you are *fleshing it out*. To *flesh out* is to expand something or build it up.

- **Let's** flesh out **this proposal and make it more meaty.**
- **We need an all-day meeting to** flesh out **these ideas.**

When you shoo a flock of birds out of hiding, you are *flushing them out*. *Flush out* is also a metaphor for revealing things or clearing them out.

- **The hunters** flushed out **their prey.**
- **Let's** flush out **that politician's real backers.**

Flounder Versus Founder

Founder means to fail completely or sink.

> **The pumps will buy you time, but minutes only. From this moment on, no matter what we do, Titanic will** founder.
>
> —Victor Garber playing Thomas Andrews
> in the movie *Titanic*

Flounder means to be confused and thrash around clumsily.

> **Families found their sons to be different from the boys who had marched off to war. Some of them were eager to assume the responsibilities of life, while others** floundered, **determined to make up for the years they had lost.**
>
> —Earl Hamner Jr. as the narrator
> in the TV show *The Waltons*

These words probably come from the same root, and when a horse stumbles or goes lame it is said to *founder* instead of *flounder*, as would be expected.

QUICK AND DIRTY TIP

A *flounder* is also a kind of fish, so in general, you can remember that fish thrash around clumsily—*flounder*—when out of their element.

Foreword Versus Forward

Books have **forewords**. *Foreword* is made by combining the prefix *fore-* with *word*, giving the literal meaning "before the word"—the introduction before the main words of a book.

Things or people move **forward** (to the front), are *forward* (brash or bold), or are *forward* thinking (modern and progressive), just to list a few examples. *Foreword* is only a noun—a type of introduction to a book. *Forward* can be many parts of speech.

> **The farther backward you can look, the farther** forward **you can see.**
>
> —Winston Churchill

Forward is the older of the two words, coming from Old English, a time before books were printed. *Forward* is made by combining the word *fore* with the suffix *-ward*. *-Ward* means "direction," so *forward* means "in the fore direction."

Although *forwards* (with an *s*) is still used in British English, *forward* is the correct American English spelling.

QUICK AND DIRTY TIP

Books contain words, and the spelling of the type of *foreword* you see in books ends with *word*.

Former Versus Latter

Former and **latter** let you refer to things in a previous phrase or sentence.

Use these terms only when distinguishing between two choices, and use them sparingly because they confuse many people. Even if your readers know the meaning, they have to go back to the previous sentence to find the answer:

> **The carpenter and the geometer look for the right angle, but in different ways: the** former **only wants such an approximation to it as his work requires, but the** latter **wants to know what constitutes a right angle or what is its special quality; his aim is to find out the truth.**
>
> —Aristotle

Often the sentence is easier to follow if you simply use the same words again:

> **The carpenter and the geometer look for the right angle, but in different ways: the** carpenter **only wants such an approximation to it as his work requires, but the** geometer **wants to know what constitutes a right angle or what is its special quality; his aim is to find out the truth.**

Avoid *former* and *latter* in speech because listeners can't go back and review what you said in the previous sentence (and if they try, they'll probably miss what you say next).

QUICK AND DIRTY TIP

Latter means "last" (note that both start with *l*) and *former* means "first" (note that both start with *f*).

Gorilla Versus Guerrilla

Unless you're hawking primates, you're not engaging in **go-rilla** marketing. It's **guerrilla** marketing.

The term *guerrilla* comes from a Spanish word that means "little war." *Guerrilla* fighters typically launch small, targeted attacks as opposed to the large military campaigns typically run by nations. Similarly, *guerrilla* marketers use targeted, creative marketing methods as opposed to the expensive, traditional campaigns run by large corporations.

> **Apparently they strayed off course. And we're fairly certain they're in** guerrilla **hands.**
>
> —R. G. Armstrong playing Major General Phillips in the movie *Predator*

Gorillas are indigenous to the forests of central Africa and are the largest of the primates—males can weigh up to 500 pounds.

> **Space. It seems to go on and on forever. But then you get to the end and a** gorilla **starts throwing barrels at you.**
>
> —Billy West voicing Philip J. Fry in the TV show *Futurama*

Hangar Versus Hanger

You hang clothes or pictures on a **hanger**.

> **No wire** hangers**, ever.**
>
> —Faye Dunaway playing Joan Crawford
> in the movie *Mommie Dearest*

You park planes or spaceships in a hangar. **Hangar** comes from the French word for "shed."

> **Yeah. We're spending [our first weekend in Europe] in an airplane** hangar **. . . guarding a truck!**
>
> —Bill Murray playing John Winger
> in the movie *Stripes*

QUICK AND DIRTY TIP

When you put something on a *hanger*, you are literally a *hanger*, a person who hangs something, just like a play<u>er</u> plays, a sing<u>er</u> sings, and a writ<u>er</u> writes.

Hanged Versus Hung

Oddly, there are two past-tense forms of the verb *hang*. **Hanged** is for people and animals you intend to kill, and **hung** is for everything else.

Remember to use *hanged* to talk about killing people by dangling them from a rope by thinking of the Old West. Hangings were common, and "I'll be *hanged*" was a common exclamation. Think of a prospector expressing surprise about being framed for a crime by saying, "I'll be *hanged*!" He's using it as an exclamation, and he's probably literally correct.

> **I am bewitched with the rogue's company.**
> **If the rascal have not given me medicines**
> **to make me love him, I'll be** hanged.
>
> —Falstaff referring to his friend Poins
> in Shakespeare's *Henry IV*

You can remember that *hung* is for things such as curtains, disco balls, and stockings by thinking of a line from "'Twas The Night Before Christmas": "The stockings were hung by the chimney with care."

The ships hung **in the sky in much the same way that bricks don't.**

—*The Hitchhiker's Guide to the Galaxy*
by Douglas Adams

We have to deal with two forms because there were at least two separate words for *hang* in Old English. They eventually merged into one, but the separate past tense forms remained. *Hung* became the word for most uses, but the losing form (*hanged*) stuck around for executions, probably because it was used in legal language, which is less likely to change than common language.

Heroin Versus Heroine

Who knew that **heroin** was originally the name of a legal drug sold in the late 1800s by Bayer? It comes from a German word that means "powerful." They didn't know the half of it!

Heroin, the drug, is spelled without an *e*.

> **It's your scent. It's like a drug to me. It's like you're my own personal brand of heroin.**
>
> —Robert Pattinson as the vampire Edward Cullen in the movie *Twilight*

Heroine, the woman who saves the day in your next novel, is spelled with an *e*.

> **Uh-oh. This does not look good for our heroine.**
>
> —David Boreanaz as Angelus in the TV show *Buffy the Vampire Slayer*

QUICK AND DIRTY TIP

Remember the spelling by thinking that the *heroine* in your favorite novel has that extra something about her, that extra pizzazz that makes everyone love her—and the word *heroine* has that extra *e* on the end.

Hilarious
Versus Hysterical

When you're rolling on the floor laughing, describe the joke as **hilarious**, not **hysterical**.

Hilarious means roughly "super funny"; it comes from a Greek word meaning "cheerful."

> **So, aside from coming up with your** hilarious **one-liners, what's your next move?**
>
> —Alan Dale playing Caleb in the TV show *The O.C.*

Hysterical means "excited." It comes from the same root as *hysteria*, a Greek word meaning "womb" (coming from the old idea—hrumph—that only women are emotionally excitable). Some kinds of laughter can be *hysterical*. If people are so uncomfortable that they laugh in an inappropriate situation, such as at a funeral or while being robbed, that is likely *hysterical* laughter.

> **Return the shoes? I can't talk to you when you're** hysterical**.**
>
> —Eva Longoria playing Gabrielle in the TV show *Desperate Housewives*

QUICK AND DIRTY TIP

Think of <u>hyster</u>ectomy when you think of <u>hyster</u>ical. A woman who needs a hysterectomy is likely to be upset, and that's not funny.

Historic
Versus Historical

Historic is an adjective describing something important or influential in history: *Many people viewed it as a* historic *occasion when the Dow Jones Industrial Average hit 10,000 for the first time.*

> **Take a good look, my dear. It's an** historic **moment you can tell your grandchildren about—how you watched the Old South fall one night.**
>
> —Clark Gable playing Rhett Butler in the movie
> *Gone with the Wind*

Historical is an adjective that refers to anything from the past, important or not: *You can find* historical *stock prices online.*

> **These are facts,** historical **facts, not schoolbook history, not Mr. Wells' history, but history nevertheless.**
>
> —Sydney Greenstreet playing Kasper Gutman in the
> movie *The Maltese Falcon*

QUICK AND DIRTY TIP

Think of the *al* at the end of *historical* as standing for *all in the past.*
Think of the *ic* at the end of *historic* as standing for *important.*

Hoard Versus Horde

The verb *to* **horde** means "to gather or congregate in a large group." It's more common to hear *horde* used as a noun, though, to describe a mass or mob of people or animals. *Horde* came to English by way of multiple foreign languages. The oldest form may be a Turkic word for "camp." *Horde* is still the Danish word for "troop."

> **Society is now one polished** horde, **formed of two mighty tribes, the Bores and Bored.**
>
> —Lord Byron, British poet

To **hoard** is to amass a large quantity of something or a stash of something valuable or scarce. *Hoard* comes to English from a Goth word for "treasure," and if you've seen the TV show *Hoarders*, which debuted in 2009, you'll know that treasure can be bad thing.

> **If more of us valued food and cheer and song above** hoarded **gold, it would be a merrier world.**
>
> —J. R. R. Tolkien

QUICK AND DIRTY TIP

If you're part of a *horde*, you'll likely be bored. Note the similarity in spelling between *horde* and *bored*. The spellings aren't exactly the same, but neither has an *a* like *hoard*.

Home Versus Hone

To get closer to finding a difficult truth and a hiding criminal, you **home** in on them, just as a *homing* device allows you to find something.

> **And you're sure the** homing **beacon is secure onboard their ship? I'm taking an awful risk, Vader.**
>
> —Peter Cushing playing Grand Moff Tarkin in the movie *Star Wars: Episode IV—A New Hope*

Hone means to sharpen and comes from an Old English word that meant "stone" or "rock"—you *hone* a knife on a sharpening stone.

> **With the solve rate for murders at about twenty percent, Miami is a great place for me. A great place for me to** hone **my craft. Viva Miami.**
>
> —Michael C. Hall playing Dexter Morgan in the TV show *Dexter*

QUICK AND DIRTY TIP

Think of a *homing* pigeon homing in on its destination to remember that you *home* (not *hone*) in on something.

I Versus Me

The simple little pronouns **I** and **me** often give people fits when they're combined with other pronouns or names in a sentence.

I is a subject pronoun, so you use it when you are the subject of a sentence—the one taking action.

> **That fight . . . it was the first honest interaction you and I have had since we came back to work.**
>
> —Lisa Edelstein playing Dr. Lisa Cuddy
> in the TV show *House*

Me is an object pronoun, so you use it when you are the object of a sentence—the one receiving an action—or when the pronoun follows a preposition such as *between, of,* or *over.*

Only a person who wanted to find the Stone—find it, but not use it—would be able to get it. That is one of my more brilliant ideas. And between you and me, that is saying something.

—Richard Harris playing Albus Dumbledore in the movie *Harry Potter and the Sorcerer's Stone*

QUICK AND DIRTY TIP

Consider which pronoun you would use if it were the only one in the clause. That's still the one you want even if there are other people in the sentence, and it's usually easier to see the right choice that way.

Impact

Although **impact** has taken root in the business world as a verb, as in *Cutting prices will impact our revenue,* many people maintain that *impact* is proper only as a noun, meaning "effect."

> **At a time when the public is rightly concerned about the** impact **of sex and violence on TV, this administration is gonna protect the MUPPETS!**
>
> —Richard Schiff playing Toby Ziegler
> in the TV show *The West Wing*

Objectors believe that the verb *impact* means only "to hit," and any other use is just irritating jargon. Usually when you are tempted to use *impact* as a verb, *affect* is the better choice.

> **You don't let other people's problems** affect **you. You don't let your own problems** affect **you. And it's the problems that make us interesting.**
>
> —Jesse Spencer playing Dr. Robert Chase
> on the TV show *House*

QUICK AND DIRTY TIP

If you can put an article such as *an* or *the* in front of *impact,* you are using it in the most proper way—as a noun.

Imply Versus Infer

Implying is something done by writers or speakers. Inferring is something done by listeners or readers.

When you **imply**, you hint at something rather than saying it directly. *Imply* comes from an Old French word that meant "to enfold." You can think of an *implied* statement as hidden, or folded, into what was actually said.

> **I've got a great cigar collection—it's actually not a collection, because that would** imply **I wasn't going to smoke every last one of 'em.**
>
> —Ron White, comedian

When you **infer**, you deduce some meaning that was left unsaid. *Infer* comes from a Latin word that means "to bring in." You can think of readers or listeners using their own interpretation to bring into a sentence a meaning that isn't explicitly stated.

> **We** infer **the spirit of the nation in great measure from the language.**
>
> —Ralph Waldo Emerson

The incorrect use of *infer* to mean *imply* is so common that in a decade or so it may be considered standard, but for now, careful writers and speakers continue to make a distinction.

Infamous
Versus Notorious

Infamous is a negative thing. If you're *infamous*, you have a bad reputation.

> **Once you become famous, there is nothing left to become but** infamous

> —Don Johnson, American actor

Notorious can be positive or negative. If you're *notorious*, it may mean you're well known for something good or for something bad.

> **Books about the law are** notorious **for being very long, very dull, and very difficult to read. This is one reason many lawyers make heaps of money.**

> —*A Series of Unfortunate Events: The Bad Beginning* by Lemony Snicket

Be careful when using *notorious*: Since it can connote either good or bad, your meaning may be unclear. If you say Squiggly's cupcakes are *notorious,* for example, it's unclear whether they are delicious or horrible. It's clearer to say Squiggly's cupcakes are *notorious* for their moistness or for their ability to break teeth.

Inflammable
Versus Flammable

Flammable means that something burns easily. **Inflammable** means the same thing and is the original word, but many people mistakenly believe it means resistant to burning. The prefix *in-* commonly has a negative meaning, but in *inflammable,* it acts as an intensifier just as it does in words such as *intoxicate* and *indent.*

It's best to avoid *inflammable*—it's a safety issue.

> Inflammable **means** flammable? **What a country.**
>
> —Hank Azaria voicing Dr. Nick Riviera
> in the TV show *The Simpsons*

Invaluable
Versus **Valuable**

Something **invaluable** has worth beyond calculation. It's priceless.

> **You have invented a very useful young brother called Ernest, in order that you may be able to come up to town as often as you like. I have invented an** invaluable **permanent invalid called Bunbury, in order that I may be able to go down into the country whenever I choose.**
>
> —*The Importance of Being Earnest* by Oscar Wilde

It's possible to put a price on something that is merely **valuable**.

> **Sincerity of utterance is** valuable **in a critic, but sanity of judgment is more** valuable **still.**
>
> —*Reviews* by Oscar Wilde

Ironic

Irony is difficult to define, but you know it when you see it. What's **ironic** in one situation or to one person is not necessarily *ironic* in all situations or to all people, because irony is related to the expected outcome or behavior. A guy in a lime green leisure suit at a disco in the 1970s was normal. A guy in a lime green leisure suit at a high school dance today is *ironic*. It's all about what's expected. Our 1970s dancer was going with the fashion of the day by wearing an expected outfit. Our current dancer is attempting to make some kind of rebellious statement by wearing an unexpected outfit.

> **Sometimes the dude with the horn-rimmed glasses and the Smurfs T-shirt is being** ironic**, and sometimes he's just a dork who has a love-hate relationship with Gargamel.**
>
> —Cobie Smulders playing Robin Scherbatsky in the TV show *How I Met Your Mother*

Irony comes from the Greek word for "dissembler" and is used to describe a situation in which something is the opposite of what you expect or what the speaker means.

> **Yes, my sister and I were actually a very good team. We were called "fire and nice." I was "fire," 'cause of the red hair, and Claire was "nice," because it was** ironic **and she wasn't.**
>
> —Jesse Tyler Ferguson playing Mitchell Pritchett in the TV show *Modern Family*

Irregardless
Versus Regardless

Irregardless may be the most hated word in the English language. Don't use it. Trust me. Just put down the *ir* and back away.

Regardless is the word you want. It's already negative. Putting *ir* in front of it creates a word that means "not without regard."

Language experts think *irregardless* probably arose because people weren't sure whether the word they wanted was *irrespective* or *regardless*. Alternatively, people could have been modeling the made-up word after the many English words that start with *irre: irrelevant, irrespective, irresistible,* and so on. *Regardless* of the reason it exists, avoid *irregardless*.

Lay Versus Lie

You need to know about subjects and objects to figure out when to use **lay** and **lie**. Subjects are the ones taking action. Objects are the targets of an action.

Lie is the subject verb. Use it when you or the person or thing you are writing about is doing something.

> **I just wanna lie on the beach and eat hot dogs. That's all I've ever wanted.**
>
> —Brian Baumgartner playing Kevin Malone
> in the TV show *The Office*

Lay is the object verb. Use it when someone or something is being acted on—put down or moved—by someone or something else. (And just to make things complicated, *lay* is also the past tense of *lie*.)

> **If you lay a finger on Phyllis, I'll kill you.**
>
> —Steve Carell playing Michael Scott
> in the TV show *The Office*

QUICK AND DIRTY TIP

Everyone knows hens *lay* eggs. Think of eggs as the object, and think of this sentence that uses both words properly: *Hens* lie *down to* lay *eggs.*

Lightening
Versus Lightning

Back in the 1300s nobody paid much attention to spelling, and you wouldn't even recognize some of the letters our Middle English ancestors used. Back then, everyone used the same word for **lightening** (making something lighter) and **lightning** (bolts of light from the sky), so you can be forgiven for mixing them up today. Forgiven? Yes. Let off the hook? No.

Lightening (with an *e*) means "to lighten something." It's what you do to your hair with bleach.

Lightning (without an *e*) means "a bolt of light from the sky."

Lightning can also be a metaphor for something fast: *Lightning* McQueen was the name of one of the racers in the movie *Cars*, and games and TV programs have been known to have a *lightning* round. One of the earliest shows to have a *lightning*

round was the game show *Password* in 1961, and more recently, CNBC's *Mad Money* and ESPN's *Around the Horn* have a *lightning* round.

> **The difference between the right word and the almost right word is a really large matter—it's the difference between** lightning **and a** lightning **bug.**
>
> —Mark Twain

QUICK AND DIRTY TIP

Remember that *lightning* is spelled without an *e* by imagining a *lightning* bolt zapping the *e* from the word.

Lend Versus Loan

In Britain, **lend** is the verb and **loan** is the noun.

> **Good advice is never as helpful as an interest-free** loan.
>
> —Mason Cooley, American professor and writer

In the United States, most language experts consider the words interchangeable when you are talking about money or items. Nevertheless, some sticklers disagree, and if you wish to avoid their scolding, stick to the British rules.

> **Everybody likes a kidder, but nobody** lends **him money.**
>
> —Arthur Miller, American playwright and essayist

QUICK AND DIRTY TIP

Remember that *loan* and *noun* both have an *o* in them, and *lend* and *verb* both have an *e* in them.

Loath Versus Loathe

Loath (without an *e*) is an adjective, meaning it is used like *sad* or *eager,* and it means "reluctant." You can be sad to admit something, eager to admit something, or *loath* to admit something.

> **PRINCE HAL: Why, thou owest God a death.**
>
> **FALSTAFF: 'Tis not due yet; I would be** loath
> **to pay him before his day.**
>
> —*The First Part of King Henry IV*
> by William Shakespeare

Loathe is a verb, meaning it is used like "hate" or "overlook." You can hate bad grammar, overlook bad grammar, or *loathe* bad grammar.

> **I** loathe **people who keep dogs. They are**
> **cowards who haven't got the guts to bite**
> **people themselves.**
>
> —August Strindberg, Swedish writer

Both words are related to the Old English word that meant "hostile."

QUICK AND DIRTY TIP

Think that *loathe* (the verb) ends in *e*, and the only vowel in *verb* is *e*. Therefore, the *e* on the end of *loathe* signals *verb*.

Loose Versus Lose

Notice that when you say **loose** (the word that is the opposite of *tight*), you place more emphasis on the *o* than when you say **lose** (the word that is the opposite of *win* and *find*). The word with more emphasis on the *o* has more *o*'s. Voila! Now you can remember how to spell the two.

> **If I'm forced to choose between you and me, guess what? You** lose!
>
> —Rutina Wesley playing Tara Thornton in the TV show *True Blood*

> **How do I know this isn't another dream? Wait a minute. All my teeth are** loose. **This is real.**
>
> —Tracy Morgan playing Tracy Jordan on the TV show *30 Rock*

QUICK AND DIRTY TIP

A common phrase is *loose as a goose*, and both *loose* and *goose* are spelled with two *o*'s.

Momentarily
Versus in a Moment

Around 100 years ago, the proper use of **momentarily** was to mean "**for a moment**."

> **If we stop** momentarily **for gas, we can still make the 10:00 flight to Phoenix.**

Today, the use of *momentarily* to mean "in a moment" is common—so common that it's in most dictionaries, although some label it as problematic.

> **The plane will be landing** momentarily.
> **Welcome to Phoenix.**

It's not widely considered wrong to use *momentarily* in that way, but you should know that some people may object to it based on historical distinctions. This is the safe way to say it:

> **The plane will be landing** in a moment.
> **Welcome to Phoenix.**

Moral <small>Versus</small> Morale

Morale is a feeling of mental or emotional confidence. Someone with good *morale* is optimistic and cheerful, whereas someone with poor *morale* is dejected or downtrodden.

> **I intend to assist in the effort to reestablish communication with Starfleet. However, if crew morale is better served by my roaming the halls weeping, I will gladly defer to your medical expertise.**
>
> —Zachary Quinto playing Spock
> in the movie *Star Trek*

Morals refer to beliefs about right and wrong. For example, the *moral* of a story is the lesson it teaches about proper behavior. *Moral* is also an adjective that relates to principles of proper behavior—a *moral* victory, a *moral* duty, or a *moral* dilemma, for example.

> **The higher the buildings, the lower the morals.**
>
> —Noël Coward, British writer and entertainer

Me Versus Myself

Myself is what's usually called a reflexive pronoun. You can remember the name *reflexive* by thinking that when you look in a mirror, you see your reflection. You'd say, "I see *myself* in the mirror," and that's the right way to use *myself*: to "reflect back" on an earlier mention of yourself in the sentence.

> **I made the jelly beans** myself. (Myself
> reflects back on the earlier I.)

Me is the pronoun you want when you are in the object position in a sentence—the target of an action.

> **Sam sent the jelly beans to** me. (Me **is the
> object—the target of the sending.)**

People seem to become confused when there is more than one object, but it doesn't matter whether you are the only target of an action or part of a group. *Me* is the right choice, not *myself*.

> **Sam sent the jelly beans to Joe, Howard,
> Pat, and** me.

Me, My, and Gerunds

Sometimes a gerund (an -*ing* form of a verb; it acts like a noun) takes an object pronoun such as **me** or *him,* and sometimes a gerund takes a possessive pronoun such as **my** or *his.*

In some sentences the distinction is more clear than in others. The difference in meaning should be obvious here:

> **What do you think of** me **running for president?**

> **What do you think of** my **running for president?**

In the first sentence, the emphasis is on the person who is running. It means something like *What do you think of me running for president instead of Bob.* In the second sentence, it's clear that you are already running for president and want to know what the reader thinks of that situation. Some sentences are more tricky:

> **Do you mind** my **whipping up a latte while you're trying to study?**

> **Do you mind** me **whipping up a latte while you're trying to study?**

Me, My, and Gerunds

QUICK AND DIRTY TIP

Usually you want the possessive. Choose the right pronoun by considering what you're implying. When you ask if someone minds *"me* whipping up a latte," you're asking if he objects to you. When you ask if someone minds *"my* whipping up a latte," you're asking if he objects to the noisy act of running the milk steamer.

Nauseated
Versus Nauseous

Both **nauseous** and **nauseated** are derived from a Greek word for "seasickness."

To nauseate means "to sicken."

> **You nauseate me, Mr. Grinch.**
>
>> —from a song in the TV special *How the Grinch Stole Christmas!*

Conservative language folks believe that *nauseous* should be used only to mean "to induce nausea" or "nausea inducing." Things that make you sick are *nauseous*.

> **You** nauseate **me, Mr. Grinch / With a** nauseous **super-naus.**
>
>> —from a song in the TV special *How the Grinch Stole Christmas!*

When you feel sick, you are *nauseated*. Nevertheless, people use *nauseous* to mean *nauseated* so often that some style guides now consider it standard. In twenty years, we'll probably drop this entry from the book, but for now, reserve *nauseous* to mean something that makes you sick, not to describe how you feel.

Peak Versus Peek Versus Pique

Pique, from a French word meaning "prick," means "to excite." You want to excite people's interest.

> **Nothing** piques **my interest more than repeated failure.**
>
> —Richard Dean Anderson playing Jack O'Neill in the TV show *Stargate SG-1*

Peeking is looking when you shouldn't.

> **Oh, I wasn't a perfect gentleman. I might have snuck a** peek.
>
> —James Denton playing Mike Delfino in the TV show *Desperate Housewives*

A **peak** is a real or metaphorical high point or pinnacle.

> **Hey, well, as far as I'm concerned, progress** peaked **with frozen pizza.**
>
> —Bruce Willis playing John McClane in the movie *Die Hard 2*

QUICK AND DIRTY TIP

Think of the two *e*'s in *peek* as two eyes *peeking*.

Precede Versus Proceed

To **precede** is to come before something else.

> **It seems my reputation had** preceded **me here.**
>
> —Jon Favreau playing Mike
> in the movie *Swingers*

To **proceed** is to go on or continue.

> **But then she reaches in her bag and pulls out a strawberry Pop-Tart—the very same breakfast pastry I was consuming at that moment! What was I to do? How was I to** proceed**?**
>
> —Ethan Embry playing Preston Meyers
> in the movie *Can't Hardly Wait*

QUICK AND DIRTY TIP

Remember that the prefix *pre-* means "comes before."

Principal
Versus Principle

Principal and **principle** are both nouns, but only *princi-pal* can also be an adjective. The most common meaning of *principal* as an adjective is "main, or highest in rank or impor-tance," as in *My* principal *complaint is a persistent headache.*

As a noun, the word *principal* has more than ten meanings, including the head of a school, the noninterest portion of a loan, and an important person such as the star of a movie or a business owner.

> **A lot of educators tell students, "Think of your** principal **as your pal." I say, "Think of me as your judge, jury, and executioner."**
>
> —Armin Shimerman playing Principal Synder in the TV show *Buffy the Vampire Slayer*

Principle refers to a fundamental law, doctrine, tenet, or ideal. You could use it to refer to grammatical *principles,* meaning rules, or you could say that someone is a man of *principle,* meaning he has strong ideals.

> **Her name alone invokes awe. Faith. A set of** principles **or beliefs upon which you're willing to devote your life.**
>
> —Tom Lenk playing Andrew Wells in the TV show *Buffy the Vampire Slayer*

Prostate Versus Prostrate

My father always says **prostrate** when he means **prostate**. He also says the guacamole he gets in the winter is from "down south, in Guacamolia," which is a lot funnier than the *prostate* mix-up.

To *prostrate* oneself is to lie facedown to symbolize subservience, humility, overwhelming adoration, or, sometimes, exhaustion. Pilgrims often *prostrate* themselves before major religious shrines.

The *prostate* is a male gland. When a man gets to a certain age, he gets his *prostate* examined regularly.

Annoyingly, my father isn't the only one who's confused: A Google search for *prostrate* is likely to return at least as many articles about cancer as it does about people showing devotion.

QUICK AND DIRTY TIP

Prostate comes from a Latin root word that means "to stand before" because the *prostate* gland "stands before" the bladder. It's possible for a man to stand up while having his *prostate* examined. Note that *stand* starts with *sta*, which is the syllable in *prostate* that often confuses people: You can <u>sta</u>nd when you have your pro<u>sta</u>te examined.

Purposely
Versus Purposefully

Purposely is the word you want when describing something done deliberately—done *on purpose*. If you know your sister is always late, you may *purposely* tell her the party starts thirty minutes earlier than it really does.

> **A lot of times when a package says "Open Other End," I** purposely **open the end where it says that.**
>
> —George Carlin, American comedian

Purposefully describes the action or demeanor of a person who is determined or resolute. If you want to convey a message to your brother without speaking, you may *purposefully* raise your eyebrows.

> **To associate with other like-minded people in small,** purposeful **groups is for the great majority of men and women a source of profound psychological satisfaction.**
>
> —Aldous Huxley

QUICK AND DIRTY TIP

Think of *purposefully* (purpose-full-y) as "full of *purpose*."

Quotation
Versus Quote

Quotation is a noun.

> **I hate** quotations. **Tell me what you know.**
>> —Ralph Waldo Emerson, American writer

Quote is a verb.

> **Famous remarks are very seldom** quoted **correctly.**
>> —Simeon Strunsky, American essayist

It's common to hear people use the verb *quote* as a shortened form of *quotation*, but in the strictest sense, this use is wrong.

Raise Versus Raze

Raise and **raze** have the same pronunciation but very opposite meanings.

Raise means "to lift up, build, or grow." It comes from an Old English word that meant "rear," as in "to rear a child."

> **DWIGHT SCHRUTE: Through concentration, I can** raise **and lower my cholesterol at will.**
>
> **PAM BEESLY: Why would you want to** raise **your cholesterol?**
>
> **DWIGHT SCHRUTE: So I can lower it.**
>
> —Rainn Wilson playing Dwight and Jenna Fischer playing Pam in the TV show *The Office*

Raze comes from a Latin word that means "to scrape," and it's the word you use to describe knocking down or leveling buildings.

> **If I ever learned that insurrection had spread across my ranks, if I ever discovered that my men had aligned themselves against me, I would** raze **this planet.**

—Callum Blue playing Major Zod
in the TV show *Smallville*

QUICK AND DIRTY TIP

Raze is related to the word *razor*, so you can think that *razing* a building makes the landscape smooth in the same way that using a razor on your body makes your skin smooth.

Reign Versus Rein

To **reign** is to rule, prevail, or hold dominion over something, for example, as a king or the winner of a contest. Like many words relating to government and monarchy, *reign* comes to English from French.

> **At 20 years of age the will** reigns, **at 30 the wit, at 40 the judgment.**
>
> —Benjamin Franklin

Literally, **reins** are the straps you use to steer an animal such as a horse. Metaphorically, *reins* can be anything used to exert control or restraint. *Rein* comes from a Latin word that means "to hold back."

> **If passion drives you, let reason hold the** reins.
>
> —Benjamin Franklin

QUICK AND DIRTY TIP

Remember to put the *g* in *reign* by reminding yourself that kings and queens are regal and wear regalia, both of which have a *g*.

Regime Versus Regimen Versus Regiment

A **regime**, sometimes spelled with an accented *e* (*régime*), is a type of government or ruling structure.

> **There is a totalitarian** regime **inside every one of us.**
>
> —Eric Hoffer, American writer and philosopher

A **regimen** is a course of behavior or treatment. Your doctor may recommend a diet or exercise *regimen*.

> **The one thing more difficult than following a** regimen **is not imposing it on others.**
>
> —Marcel Proust, French writer

A **regiment** is a group of military forces. It comes from the Latin word for "government."

> **What makes a** regiment **of soldiers a more noble object of view than the same mass of mob? Their arms, their dresses, their banners, and the art and artificial symmetry of their position and movements.**
>
> —Lord Byron, British poet

Reluctant Versus Reticent

Reluctant means unwilling or disinclined.

> **Do not ask the name of the person who seeks a bed for the night. He who is reluctant to give his name is the one who most needs shelter.**
>
> —*Les Misérables* by Victor Hugo

Reticent comes from the Latin word for "silent." It has been misused so often that some dictionaries now include "reluctant" as one of its meanings, but its primary meaning is to "be silent, restrained, or reserved." Careful writers reserve it for such uses.

> **I do not know why Captain Nichols left England. It was a matter upon which he was reticent, and with persons of his kind a direct question is never very discreet.**
>
> —*The Moon and Sixpence* by William Somerset Maugham

QUICK AND DIRTY TIP

Reticent and *silent* both have an *i*.

Riffle Versus Rifle

Both **riffle** and **rifle** mean to go through something, but there's a subtle difference.

When you're *riffling*, you're hastily flipping through something —such as book pages—or shuffling cards. *Riffle* is thought to be a blend between *ripple* and *ruffle*.

> **The Riffle Shuffle: This is the shuffle ordinarily used by card players, but in spite of its almost universal use, it is rarely done neatly or even smoothly. Nearly always the cards are bent far too much and then pushed together clumsily.**
>
> —*The Royal Road to Card Magic* by Jean Hugard

When you're rifling, you're searching frantically or ransacking, usually to steal something. *Rifle* is from the Old French word for "steal or plunder."

> **We don't just borrow words; on occasion, English has pursued other languages down alleyways to beat them unconscious and** rifle **their pockets for new vocabulary.**
>
> —James D. Nicoll, American Usenet personality

QUICK AND DIRTY TIP

The word that is spelled like the gun—*rifle*—is the one you use when you are committing a crime.

Segue Versus Segway

A curse upon Dean Kamen. I hear he's a nice man who has helped the world, but he is also the inventor of the **Segway** upright, two-wheeled, electric transportation thingy favored by mall cops. In an attempt to be cute, his company gave the contraption a name that's a funny spelling of **segue**—a word that means "smooth transition." Given that high-tech companies have more marketing money than language experts who, say, like the word *segue,* when writers think "*segue*" now, they often see *s-e-g-w-a-y* in their minds.

Segue is an Italian word that got its start as a description on a musical score to indicate that the musician should continue in some way—that the musician should make a smooth transition between the parts. Today *segue* is used to describe many kinds of transitions. Radio and TV announcers often talk about the *segue* between topics, for example.

> **THE DOCTOR: I plan to** segue **from Don Juan to Rigoletto in the blink of an eye. It will be a triumph of . . .**
> **B'Elanna Torres: Arrogance and self-absorption?**
>
> —Robert Picardo (The Doctor) and Roxann Dawson (B'Elanna Torres) in the TV show *Star Trek: Voyager*

QUICK AND DIRTY TIP

Whenever you need to use the word *segue*, remember its foreign-feeling spelling by remembering that it comes from music and by imagining an Italian composer. When you want to write about the personal transportation unit, remember that it ends with the word *way* by imagining Dean Kamen pointing for you to go "that way."

Set Versus Sit

Sit is for actions; it does not require an object.

> **There are two kinds of folks who** sit **around thinking about how to kill people: psychopaths and mystery writers. I'm the kind that pays better.**
>
> —Nathan Fillion playing Richard Castle
> in the TV show *Castle*

Set, on the other hand, is what you do with things. *Set* requires an object.

> **I accidentally** set **a python on my cousin Dudley at the zoo once. Once. But so what? I bet loads of people here can do it.**
>
> —Daniel Radcliffe playing Harry Potter
> in the movie *Harry Potter and
> the Chamber of Secrets*

QUICK AND DIRTY TIP

When you're training a dog, you tell her to *sit*. That is how you use *sit*—for the action of sitting, like a dog plopping its bottom on the ground.

Silicon Versus Silicone

Silicon and **silicone** are both chemistry terms.

Silicon is element 14 in the period table of elements. It's found in the ground in materials such as sand, clay, quartz, granite, and mica. Computer chips rely on *silicon,* which is why people call the San Francisco Bay Area—the home of the computer chip and the epicenter of chip companies—*Silicon* Valley.

> **Whether we are based on carbon or** silicon **makes no fundamental difference. We should each be treated with appropriate respect.**
>
> —Bob Balaban playing Dr. Chandra in the movie
> *2010: The Year We Make Contact*

Silicone is a rubbery material made by combining *silicon* with other elements such as oxygen, carbon, and hydrogen. It has a wide variety of uses. You can buy *silicone* in a tube to use as caulk; it's used in toys and hair gel, and it's popping up in all kinds of cooking items lately. I have *silicone* pot holders and baking pans, and I've been eyeing *silicone* basting brushes. It's also used in breast implants.

> **Yeah, there's no MSG in the food and there's no** silicone **in the waitresses.**
>
> —Mike O'Malley playing Jimmy
> in the TV show *Yes, Dear*

Silicon Versus Silicone

Simple Versus Simplistic

Simplistic means something is overly simplified or lacking something important. It has a negative connotation.

> **Maybe I don't have a type, Lily. God, do you think the male mind is really that simplistic? That we all have one favorite type?**
>
> —Neil Patrick Harris playing Barney Stinson
> in the TV show *How I Met Your Mother*

Simple can be good or bad. It means "basic or easy." For example, you could compliment a room for having a *simple*, clean style or a gadget for being *simple* to use. However, pretentious people can use *simple* as a put-down, and you can describe someone who is unintelligent or unsophisticated as *simple*.

> **I wanna be the person who gets happy over finding the perfect dress. I wanna be** simple, **because no one holds a gun to the head of a** simple **girl.**
>
> —Sandra Oh playing Dr. Cristina Yang
> in the TV show *Grey's Anatomy*

QUICK AND DIRTY TIP

You can think of the *ic* on the end of *simplistic* as meaning *Ick, something is missing!*

Skiddish Versus Skittish

Skiddish isn't a word. When you're describing someone who's jumpy or easily startled, the correct spelling is *skittish*—with two *t*'s.

Nobody knows for sure, but experts think *skittish* probably came from an Old Norse word that meant "to shoot."

> **Don't know about this new crew of yours. They seem a bit** skittish. **Probably shouldn't tell 'em what happened to the last crew.**
>
> —Vin Diesel playing Riddick
> in *The Chronicles of Riddick*

Skeet—a sport in which people shoot clay pigeons—also comes from an old form of *shoot* that some speculate is the same Old Norse word from which we get *skittish*.

> **Trust not a** skittish **horse, nor a great lord, when they shake their heads.**
>
> —a Danish proverb

QUICK AND DIRTY TIP

Old Norse is dictionary-speak for "We got it from the Vikings." I'd be *skittish* if I were around Vikings shooting skeet. Remember the previous sentence and note that there are no *d*'s in *skittish*, *shooting*, and *skeet*—only *t*'s.

Sneaked Versus Snuck

Sneaked and **snuck** are both past-tense forms of the verb *to sneak*. If you are in Britain or want to play it safe in America, use *sneaked*.

> **You** sneaked **out of your house? Where were you going?**
> —Robert Duncan McNeill playing Lieutenant Tom
> Paris in the TV show *Star Trek: Voyager*

Snuck has gained so much ground in the United States that some experts already say it is as acceptable as *sneaked,* and the trend is likely to continue to the point where all experts agree. Nevertheless, for now, *snuck* still irks some people, and conscientious writers and speakers avoid it.

Stationary
Versus Stationery

Stationery is paper, usually paper that you use for writing letters or notes.

> **Use the nice** stationery **to write to your grandmother.**

Stationary means "not moving, fixed in one place, still."

> **Almost every big gym has a row of** stationary **bikes.**

QUICK AND DIRTY TIP

Think of the e in stationery as standing for e-mail—the more common way that people write letters and notes these days. You can also remember that when you are stationary, you are often standing. Since standing is spelled with an a, the association can remind you to put the second a in stationary.

Supposably
Versus Supposedly

I wish I could tell you that **supposably** is not a word, but I can't. It is a word, but it doesn't mean the same thing as **supposedly** and most people use it incorrectly.

The word you usually want is *supposedly*, which means roughly "assumed to be true" and almost always includes a sense of sarcasm or disbelief.

> **Careful. This is the moment when the** supposedly **dead killer comes back to life, for one last scare.**
>
> —Jamie Kennedy playing Randy
> in the movie *Scream*

Supposably means "supposable," "conceivable," or "arguably." It's a valid word only in American English; the British wisely refuse to accept it.

> **Unless you are a professional philospher or in some other highly suppositional line of work, it is unlikely that in two lifetimes you would ever have reason to use** [supposable] **in its proper sense.**
>
> —*The Accidents of Style: Good Advice on How Not to Write Badly* by
> Charles Harrington Elster

Tack Versus Tact

Tact comes from a Latin word for "touch"—a word from which we also get the English word *tactile*. To have *tact* is to deal well with difficult or delicate situations, to have a knack for being in touch with people's needs and therefore not giving offense.

> **Miss Pascal, I think I owe you an apology. IRS agents . . . we're given rigorous aptitude tests before we can work. Unfortunately for you, we aren't tested on** tact **or good manners.**
>
> —Will Ferrell playing Harold Crick in the movie *Stranger Than Fiction*

Tack comes from a Middle English word for "attach." A *tack* is a sharp pin with a large flat head, and to *tack* something down is to fasten it with such a pin. You can also *tack* (go back and forth) when you are sailing.

> **When you try to sound like Hammond, it comes off as a hustle. I mean, it's not your fault. They say talent skips a generation. So, I'm sure your kids will be sharp as** tacks**.**
>
> —Jeff Goldblum playing Dr. Ian Malcolm in the movie *The Lost World: Jurassic Park*

Taught Versus Taut

Taught is a verb related to teaching.

> **If reality TV has** taught **us anything, it's that you can't keep people with no shame down.**
>
> —Tina Fey playing Liz Lemon in the TV show *30 Rock*

Taut means "strained or tense."

> **Enthusiasm is everything. It must be** taut **and vibrating like a guitar string.**
>
> —Pelé, Brazilian soccer player

The history of *taut* is obscure according to the *Oxford English Dictionary*, and it was spelled *taught* as recently as the 1600s; so although it's wrong today to use *taught* to mean "tight," a few hundred years ago it would have been right.

Their and They

English doesn't have a good singular pronoun to use when you don't know the sex of the person you're talking about.

> **Everyone knows** their **own Social Security number. (*Everyone* is singular, but** their **is plural.)**

In speech, people already commonly use the plural pronouns **they** and **their** in such cases, but many people object to using these words as a singular pronoun in writing (and some people even cringe when they hear it in speech).

If you wish to be cautious, use *he or she* or *his or her,* or rewrite the sentence so the subject is plural.

> **Most people know** their **own Social Security number. (*People* is plural, and** their **is plural.)**

If you choose to be bold and use *they* or *their,* you'll probably get some flak, but multiple credible style guides will back you up.

Throe Versus Throw

Throw is quite an old English word and has over fifty definitions in the *Oxford English Dictionary*. The ones you are probably most familiar with relate to propelling something through the air—*throwing* a ball, for example—but you can also *throw* a game (intentionally lose), *throw* on a dress (put it on), *throw* a pot (make it out of clay), *throw* a punch (hit someone), and more.

> "The Guide says there is an art to flying,"
> said Ford, "or rather a knack. The knack
> lies in learning how to throw yourself at the
> ground and miss."
>
> —*Life, the Universe and Everything*
> by Douglas Adams

Throe actually comes from the same root as *throw* and splintered off as its own word in the early 1600s. It means "a sharp spasm or pang of pain or emotion," and it's often expressed as a plural; for example, people are said to be in their death *throes*, the *throes* of childbirth, or the *throes* of depression.

> It was Nurse Caroline who introduced
> Homer to young Dr. Harlow, who was in
> the throes of growing out his bangs.
>
> —*The Cider House Rules* by John Irving

'Til Versus Till Versus Until

Can you **till** the land *till* the cows come home? Yes, but many people are confused about *till*, **until**, and **'til**. When you're talking about a period of time that must lapse before something happens, *till* and *until* are equivalent. *Till* has existed in English for more than a thousand years.

> **Do not bite at the bait of pleasure,** till **you know there is no hook beneath it.**
>
> —Thomas Jefferson, early American president and statesman

Until is a young'un by comparison to *till*, having arisen about three hundred years later.

> **From the moment I picked up your book** until **I laid it down, I was convulsed with laughter. Some day I intend reading it.**
>
> —Groucho Marx, American comedian

'Til is also an acceptable shortened form of *until*, but the *American Heritage Dictionary of the English Language* says the form is "etymologically incorrect."

If you want to avoid controversy, it's safest to stick with *until*.

Trooper Versus Trouper

Around the world, **troopers** are police or military men and women on horseback. In the United States, *trooper* also refers to state police officers: *He's a New York state* trooper.

> **Be honest, Scully, doesn't that propane tank bear more than a light resemblance to a little, fat, white Nazi storm** trooper?
>
> —David Duchovny playing special agent
> Fox Mulder in the TV show *The X-Files*

An acting company is a troupe (not a *troop*), so an actor in such a group is a **trouper**, and when someone powers through a tough role, he or she is a "real *trouper*."

QUICK AND DIRTY TIP

Star Wars storm *troopers*—military officers—wear white helmets with dark eyeholes. Think of the two *o*'s in *trooper* as the eyeholes in the storm *trooper* helmet.

Vain Versus Vane Versus Vein

A **vane** is a blade; you're most likely to hear the word used to refer to a weather *vane*.

> **If you send up a weather** vane **or put your thumb up in the air every time you want to do something different, to find out what people are going to think about it, you're going to limit yourself.**
>
> —Jessye Norman, American opera singer

Vain comes from an Old French word that meant "empty" or "worthless." It describes people who are full of themselves, and it's the right word to describe an act that didn't achieve its desired effect—an act done "in *vain*."

How vain **it is to sit down to write when you have not stood up to live.**

—Henry David Thoreau, American author

Vein comes from the Latin word for "blood vessel," and it describes blood vessels in English too. It can also be used to describe other types of strands, streaks, stripes, channels, or deposits, such as a *vein* of metal ore, a dark *vein* of wood through a lighter-colored wood, and one of the branching ribs in a leaf. It's also the right word to use when you're describing a mood or topic and use the phrase "in the same *vein*."

Madame you have bereft me of all words, only my blood speaks to you in my veins.

—Lord Bassanio (to Portia) in William Shakespeare's play *The Merchant of Venice*

Viola Versus Voilà

Voilà! It's what you exclaim when you have finished your masterpiece. It comes to English from French words meaning "See there!"

It's pronounced roughly "wallah," but please, please don't spell it that way. Please also don't confuse it with the **viola**: a flower that looks like a pansy, or a medium-sized instrument from the violin family. In fact, you can remember that the flower and the instrument are spelled with an *io* just like the word *violin*.

> **In the morning you go into the bathroom, a little blush, a little mascara and** voilà. **You got an old woman scared of rain.**
>
> —Ed O'Neill playing Al Bundy
> in the TV show *Married . . . with Children*

Wench Versus Winch

Wench comes from the Middle English word *wenchel,* which meant "child." A wenchel was a child of either sex, but today *wench* refers to a woman. It's most often used as a joke or an insult, but technically it can mean a country girl, a servant, a loose woman, or simply a young woman.

> **After three days men grow weary of a wench, a guest, and weather rainy.**
>
> —Benjamin Franklin in *Poor Richard's Almanack*

Winch comes from the Old English word *wince,* which meant "pully." I've used *winches* on sailboats to pull and tighten line, but a *winch* is any type of crank.

> **To the** winch, wench.
>
> —Sydney Bromley playing Engywook in the movie *The NeverEnding Story*

QUICK AND DIRTY TIP

Remember that *winch* is spelled with an *i* by associating it with the word *wince:* You may wince if you pull too hard on a *winch.*

Who Versus Whom

If you choke when confronted with the terrifying choice between **who** and **whom**, I have a cure: the him-lick maneuver. Ask if you can hypothetically answer the question with the word *him*. If you can, the right choice is *whom*. Notice that *him* and *whom* both end with the letter *m*.

For Whom **the Bell Tolls (It tolls for him.)**

If you can't answer with *him* (for example, if *he* is the word that fits), *whom* is the wrong answer—you must use *who*.

Who **is your daddy? (He is your daddy.)**

The trick works because *whom* refers to objects and *him* is an object pronoun, so *him* makes a good test case.

QUICK AND DIRTY TIP

Him equals *whom*.

Yay Versus Yea Versus Yeah

Yeah is an informal way of saying yes.

> Yeah, **we look forward to our after-game treat.**

Yea is another way of saying yes or indeed. It is most commonly used when talking about voting.

> **Ten people voted nay and three people voted** yea **on replacing oranges with pizza.**

Yay is an exclamation of excitement, joy, or happiness—it is similar to *hooray*. Remember, though, some people shout the word *yes* when they are excited too, so it's not necessarily inappropriate to use *yea* or *yeah* in such instances.

> **We'll have orange slices after the game.** Yay!

Honorable Mentions

Oh, dear. I can't stop at 101 or even 202 words. It's not enough to address all the confusion in the world, so we'll squeeze in a few more!

A lot, allot	If you have many items, you have *a lot* of items. You could *allot* them to your friends. *Alot* is not a word.
Amount, number	Use *number* for things you can count and *amount* for things you can't count.
Assure, ensure, insure	You *insure* something against financial loss, you *ensure* that some event or condition will happen, and you *assure* people their houses are safe.
Bite, byte	A short audio quotation is a sound *bite*. Computer memory is measured in *bytes*.
Calvary, cavalry	*Calvary* is a holy location; soldiers on horses are *cavalry*.
Dragged, drug	The correct past-tense form of *drag* is *dragged*.
Emigrate, immigrate	Immigrants come in; emigrants exit.
Everyday, every day	*Everyday* means "common" (the *everyday* silverware); *every day* means "each day."
Forth, fourth	You march *forth* on the *fourth* of March.

Gray, grey	*Gray* is the American spelling; *grey* is the British spelling.
Hear, here	The correct phrase is "Hear, hear!" *"Here"* is where you are.
Moose, mousse	A *moose* is an animal; a *mousse* is a fluffy dessert or a hair-styling product.
Pore, pour	You *pour* water over your plants; you *pore* over legal documents.
Shudder, shutter	The correct phrase is "*Shudder* at the thought." *Shutters* cover windows.
Steal, steel	A thief *steals* things; *steel* holds up buildings. You *steel* yourself to receive bad news.
Toe, tow	The correct phrase is "*Toe* the line." You *tow* a car.
Weather, whether	You'll walk to school *whether* the *weather* is good or bad.

Acknowledgments

Can one thank the Internet? I spent considerable time searching for just the right quotation to showcase each word in an entertaining way, and it would have taken at least ten times as long without all the wonderful, keyword-searchable Internet quotation databases. Although my searches took me far and wide, I am especially indebted to Great Quotes (great-quotes.com), the Internet Movie Database (IMDB.com), the Quotations Page (quotationspage.com), the Quotation section at Dictionary.com (http://quotes.dictionary.com/), and all the people who have highlighted favorite quotations in the Good Reads Quotation section (http://www.goodreads.com/quotes). These were my first stops for research.

For etymology research and definitions, I relied primarily on the online versions of the *Oxford English Dictionary, second*

Acknowledgments

edition, Webster's Third New International Dictionary, Unabridged, and Dictionary.com.

Thank you also to Lisa Senz at St. Martin's Press, who presented the idea for this book series; Emily Rothschild, whose editing made this a better book; Richard Rhorer, who has a hand in every part of Quick and Dirty Tips and keeps things moving smoothly; and Laurie Abkemeier, whose agenting expertise keeps me balanced, encouraged, and secure (and who contributed the *lightning* memory trick). Thank you also to Bonnie Trenga, a regular guest writer for the Grammar Girl podcast. Finally, most of all, thank you to my husband, Patrick, for being part of everything.

About the Author

Mignon Fogarty is the creator of Quick and Dirty Tips. Formerly a magazine writer, technical writer, and entrepreneur, she has a B.A. in English from the University of Washington in Seattle and an M.S. in biology from Stanford University. She lives in Reno, Nevada. Visit her Web site at quickanddirtytips.com and sign up for the free e-mail grammar tips and free podcast.

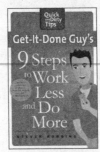
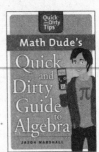

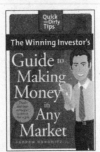